Finding

Passage

Finding

Passage

poems by

Molly Weller

PM Books

Cover photograph – Path in Yosemite National Park by John B. Weller

Born in Albany, NY in 1974, John B. Weller moved with his family to Boulder, CO in 1975. He has been photographing nature since the age of six, and his work was first published when he was eleven. Weller graduated from Stanford University with a degree in environmental economics, and then moved to Yosemite National Park before returning to Colorado to write his book on the Sand Dunes National Monument. He works as a photographer, essayist, and environmental activist. He is, also, Molly Weller's older brother.

Copyright © 2008 by Molly Weller

ISBN: 978-0-9789597-5-3

PM Books
an imprint of Poetic Matrix Press
P.O. Box 1223
Madera, CA 93639
www.poeticmatrixpress.com

Acknowledgments

Great appreciation goes to Stephen Matthews of Ginninderra Press, who published the original collection *On Finding Myself on the Map*. Great appreciation also to the Naked Knuckle, Medicinal Purposes, Poetic Matrix LettR, and the Prairie Journal (upcoming issue) for publishing some of the poems contained in this volume.

A special thanks to John Peterson of Poetic Matrix for publishing this volume and for his advice and wisdom throughout the publication process.

Heartfelt thanks to my brother, John B. Weller, for providing the photo for the cover of this book and for his endless support, encouragement, and friendship.

Thanks and Salutations to all of the colleagues, teachers, and friends who have offered me their affection, their guidance, their insight, and their unyielding friendship. To these people, I am forever grateful: David G. Brooks, Steve Jones and Nancy Dawson, Jenna Manley, Barbara McDermid, Judith Beveridge, Sue Woolfe, Geoff Page, Lynn Hard, and Nicolette Stasko.

Special thanks to William Thompson for cheerfully listening to endless drafts and for offering me his advice, his support, and his love.

To my family:

To Mom – for reading me Robert Frost when I was a kid.
To Dad – for making up bedtime stories with a little girl protagonist.
To Johnny – for being, hands down, my biggest fan
and greatest support.
To Eleanor - Rest in Peace - for believing in me and keeping
every poem and letter I ever wrote her.

Contents

Part II
Return

Finding

Passage

Part I

On Finding Myself on the Map

My Mother's Hands

The gold band
clinks
against the fork
as she cuts her meat
and the fingers
swell
from a half-glass
of wine.
They're slow
when she types
fast
when she cooks
cool
and soft
and moist from the lotion
when she smoothes hair
from my face.
I see them
among folds
of flannel,
pinching the seam,
thumb guiding
pleats
under the whirring needle.
I see them
too
holding this pen.

Of All Horrid Things, Leave Taking is the Worst
– Jane Austen

The countdown has begun
less than a month
now
three weeks
not quite
nineteen days
hours, down to
a last kiss
lips blue
with cold
moist
eager fingers
interlacing
our coupled hands merely spreading the tears.

Waiting

There is a fear
that only spreads
its blossoms to the dark,
its delicate face shying from the glare
opening moon-pale petals
to the black silk skirts
of night,
that only treads the wet avenues
of the mind
when the distance
and the waiting
and the silence
of a phone that will not ring
close down the warm
cafés of thought
leaving the street bleak
open to stalkers
the gutters full
of reflective blue-black pools.

On Finding Myself on the Map

The map lies stretched out
sleek against the cushions of the couch
light winking on its laminate.
Yellow roads scurry
over its surface,
popping out from a backdrop
of pale parks
and white-striped neighborhoods.
Glebe Island Bridge in blue
twists around one corner
through Darling Harbour
then races off the top edge
only pausing for a breath
at the Cahill Expressway.
Boxy Moore Park rounds out
into a bulbous Centennial
then slims
following Darley to the Queens.
I sit on a lower corner
hardly on the map
but there, perched
left butt cheek
covering the train station marker
a pink square
right off City Road
the noise from passing cars
vibrating its windows.

Riding without Training Wheels

In that red heat of youth
when vision does not bring
the tops of trees
and a plastic globe
stretches its raised continents
into the immensity
of imagination,
how much brighter the pain.
How it rubs raw
that hot blue bite
of first experience,
salty blood seeping
through broken skin,
eyes growing bigger
with trumpet tears.

Red on Blue

Red-rimmed papery petals
lay in mounds
on the dusky blue bed spread
and in heaps on the hardwood floor.
They fluttered down from the piping on the back
of the green velvet rocking chair,
clung wistfully to the half closed shutters.
We laughed.
That is all I remember.
Fire and ice
roses
fire and ice.

Shouldering

Low tide
sucked away from the shore,
leaving behind
turquoise pools, brimming
with creatures risking death
for a rest
from the tidal current.
The horizon
was slung
heavy with clouds.
A breeze
brought the smell of the ocean
and took back
the thick sweet smell
of us.
Skirts whipped around
first baring then concealing
pale pallid legs.
One gust caught her shell
lifted and left her
with an exposed neck
and one white arm uncovered.

Poem for N

A slender road
t-stopped
at the path.
Flowers bloomed
along its curved
length,
white and blue petals
trembling
against the black sky.
Your smell
lingers
with the blossoms
and the rain.

Baking

Counters
lie beneath a haze of flour.
Oily fingerprints
crawl
across a wooden board
and through the bits
of chocolate chips.
A silver-handled
tool of trade
finds rest for its eyelet blades
among the remains
of roasted brazil nuts,
thin dark pelts peeling back
from firm white flesh.
One curl
of filmy yellow hide
clings to the edge of a bowl
smeared with darkening batter.

City Smoke

For Ali

She blows smoke in my face
flicks ash over her shoulder
with a toss
of the wrist
perfect from practice
nonchalant
debutante
her hair reflects the light
she talks without pause
needs no encouragement
three wilted leaves
of salad
stick to her bowl
the white mug ringed with foam
and lipstick, *pretty in pink*
she tells me
in the rain
that drips reflected red
from the flowered awning.

The Bottom End of Cardigan Street

Stone stairs
angle
one from the next
around a stand
of trees
slender in their youth
and smooth.
An old fig
buckles the last step
with twisted roots,
its many branches
spreading shade
over walkway
rough walls
steep stone drive.
The smell
of over-turned earth
leaves
decaying in heaps,
the eye
in a storm.

Graveyard

White
teeth piercing
the earth
green to the gums
the flowers
like growths
of the diseases that brought them here.
The wind
steals
the skirts from her legs
strips
the flesh from her bones
almost as pale
as the sunken stones
angled
before her knees.
The bouquet
in her fingers
loses petals
into the coils of air
streaking dark patterns
across her lips.

Tears catch
on the whipping strands.

By Afternoon Light

The tips
of bare branches
broken
into twenty
squares by
the iron window.
The tree
is bursting red
blossoms.

Nightmare

The heat
slips out of the sheets
where you used to curl
around me, arm
over my ribs like a paper weight
keeping me breathing in
your scent.
The bowl
of air
where your thighs
have bowed the seat
by the window
shimmers empty,
a mirage in the blue light.
Your cup
is gone
from the cupboard
and her fingers
are in your hair.
Her lips part
from the corners,
radiating out
like an earthquake
and I
am shaking,
but you roll over
with woodpecker kisses,
my head beneath your chin
braiding my hair with your beard.

Blue Doors

1.
Moody in an autumn rain,
it swings open on its hinges
trailing drums
then slams to silence.
A drop of water slips
off the dented doorknob, brass,
onto terracotta mosaic.

2.
A vinyl chair
three-legged like the neighbor's dog
sports a deeper hue
blue
tipping towards the lost limb
on uneven pavement
sprouting grass
and a chestnut root.

3.
Duller to this fading light
the door
drifts free of the latch
tapping the tasseled handles
of a knee-high bike.
Red-lidded garbage can
overturned
across the path from the street.

4.
Tidy rows of daisies
white then yellow
line the fence
a border to the neatness
of short-clipped grass

Blue Doors continues

black and white checkered tiles
cream trimmed windows
bird-house letter box.

5.
The blue door
dusky and dim
fades into the shadows
from the leaning alder
spreading its quaking leaves
over glinting, unshuttered bays.

On a Walk in Mid-Morning Light

The air is soft
like folds of sheets
and cool
from a recent rain
clouds thread
between the buildings
reflect in wet windows
a creeper of jasmine
falls through a fence
into a gutter black with silt
its flowers bob like white buoys
in the wash.

Quilter's Burden

The table trembles on hollow legs
hinged at the middle like a knee,
bent against the weight.
Piles of cloth
lean on each other in exhaustion.
The creamy top bows and sags
strewn like the floor beneath
with half-finished projects.
An iron stands commanding,
chest puffed with dignity
defying comment on its limp cord.
A backpack, lifeless and empty,
lies still across the cutting mat.
The spool, wound tight in a navy shade,
stands pricked
by a single needle,
its empty eye
looking darkly at the room.

Cuidad de Muerto

A shelter of stone
four corners supported
by columns
of sand hued marble
streaked grey in the rain
harbors an urn
its copper plaque
now green
bleeding into the pedestal.

Boulder, CO

The town is nestled
at the base of a ring of hills
that threaten
to become mountains
if you hike too far.
Houses back-up onto
gold grassland
climbing
into solid trees
with thin limbs,
needles frosted blue,
and rocks
rubbed red and raw
from the snow.
Two gray-black
highways
break the green
one going
to the city
the second
to cracked canyons.

In My Garden That Goes On Forever

1.
The trees
drop jeweled fruit
onto the deep haze of grass.
They tower like gods
in red robes
and violet crowns.
Flower beds encircle their feet
filled with
warm tresses
and waxy limbs akimbo.
Wood fences
black from steady rain
enclose the dripping stand.

2.
One circle of grass,
in a back corner
out of sight behind the apples,
lies in blue light
reflected off the ring
of Jacob's ladder
larkspur
vervain.

3.
The peak of a pagoda
black and gold and red by my own hand
climbs out of a stand of fuchsia
and Cornus kousa
in scarlet fall bloom.
Once in full view
the Buddhist miniature,
not quite a storey,
sloping soot-grey zenith

In My Garden That Goes On Forever continues

propped up on charcoal columns,
still streams raindrops.
Silhouettes and contours
of bright dyed satin pillows
peek through shuttered windows.

4.
The foot of the garden
a fen breath of wheat-land grasses
bends and sways
on the banks
of a feeble pond
furred thick with algae and duckweed.
A scatter of corn poppy,
wine cups,
lupine.

5.
There are no boundaries to my garden
only gates.
The fences stretch their winding hides
into the ivy and the pines.

April

1

Rains come
in angled sheets, abusing
frail branches,
a weak sun sinks its shame
behind a black peak,
the sudden cold
slowing the progress of the drops
as each sprouts feathered wings,
snow flakes catch
at the web of droplets
already hung, like too many ornaments
on bare limbs
until the night breathes
a hardening freeze
into their clutching hands.

2

A peculiar ice clings
to the cherry branches
in the wet months.
The perilous embrace
of ice and limb
glows gold with the dawn,
the frozen flakes
relaxing their hold
pattering craters
into white drifts.

Cityscape

In a blossoming city
in a grove of high rise blooms
glass trees
arch their backs
thrusting their glittering bellies
towards an iron sky.

Dawn

Behind
half-burned trees
the moon
at half mast
in a sky gone pale
gone blue.

Wallabies

The ferns hung low and dense
menacing
the river.
The water gulped,
hissing
at air thick
with heat
and next day's rain.
Strands of green light
pierced the foliage
to halo a fallen log.
They came
out of the woods
like mythic beings,
exhaling the musk
of legend.

Almost Five

There is a storm
building.
The sky
has gone white
with rage.
Yellow blossoms
dance
in the first drops

are torn
in the torrent

petals dropping like rain.

Paradox

I don't care
for a calm sea
waves lapping
like a dog at the sink,
a trail of sunlines
across a rippling desert
of harmless swells,
but when an ocean
roils
and hills of water
torment the hardened cliffs,
when galloping herds
of dark clouds
scream upon the sands
their frozen daggers
pelting the foam,
when every curving lip
of beach
bares driftwood teeth
bleached blue by the wind
then
then I can see

the length of the horizon
the steady slope
of land.

Ash Blond April

Long strands of hair
hung sleek
like combed grass
along cheeks
across shoulders;
a rope
come loose of its knot,
unwound from itself,
paler
for the exposure.
Moisture clung to pink lips
a spreading pucker,
an April flower
opening in the fertile soil
of youth.
I envied her
that decade.
I pitied her
that blossom –
how far the Autumn

from that Spring.

Mid-Winter Midnight

The night
stretching silent limbs
one dark, one cold
to the panes lit
orange against that embrace,
creeping
in hoarse voice
through the cracks,
rattling its chains
under the eaves,
pools like ink
in the corners.

Red

About once a month
when the Lady's rivers flood
the sun rises red in an Eastern sky,
and the noises of the world grow so in pitch
to blend to a throbbing confusion,
I crave a steak,
like a man.
I hear him growl
from deep within the pit of my stomach,
his muscular frame pushing hard
against my rib cage
and the dimensions of my narrow shoulders.
His masculinity pulses
in my temples.
My body sheds one kind of blood,
like a tear,
while my tongue craves another,
red and rare.

Día Dolorosa

yellow steam
wafts out of the gutters
blue berries
bleed on white plates
clouds spread mouldy petals
across the sky
the rain holds back
I have a mouth
full of rotting fruit

Turtle

A round shell,
pale
banded pink
long empty of life,
snaps in two.
The one
who gave it a ragged edge,
angled now
the sun on both shoulders
dawn breaking
across bare back,
shadow falling gray
across an amethyst beach,
mountains its way to the sea.

First Cup of Tea After a Long Illness

Steam
rises tinted
green
from a cup of *Emperor's Garden*
the "Wisp of Jasmine" they claim
no wisp
but a deluge
of dew tipped flowers
their white petals blossoming
then collapsing in
upon themselves
bunches on misty stalks
rising out of the cup
swirling away
at my breath.

Chef

His eyes were tide pools
teeming with a dark life
I found myself
biting nails
running fingertips
over dry lips
gazing
lashes lowered
inappropriate messages
black lines of a tattoo
pulse across his arm
I watch him cook
steam partially obscuring his cheeks
centering his sea water eyes
bridging arched brows
thin pursed lips
smirking
my attentions
focused on blue veins
heaving up with the tendons
out of a flexed wrist
an outstretched forearm
a turned neck
supple white
eggs slip from his fingers
bounce on the edge of the toast
then sink
into a pool of flecked hollandaise
his lips twitch
on the edge of a smile
one lid is lowered
quickly withdrawn
as the plate thuds
on the table

Therapy

Finger tips
tinted saffron
grasp the amethyst
globe
as purple ringed
white petals
fall from the blade.
Green leaves
glisten
on an orange board,
waiting.
Striped prawns
curl
and blush
in a pool
of browning butter.
Therapy
taking shape
on blue plates.

Clay

It is an Oasis
this coffee shop
on Missenden
Newtown
New South Wales.
Soft black leather benches
crowd
textured tables,
their aluminum bright
next to the walls
puttied like clay.
My tea has gone cold.
Outside
black framed picture windows,
the city roars by.

In My Dreams
For my Dad

Time passes
as lethargic light
across the ripple
circling out
from my lure
and the days
move
as a bobbing
on the green wake.
Blue line
spins away
into the dark shadow
of a drop-off
before the rock
where life fans
its fins
against the current.
Rays of light
splinter
in the water.
You live
forever
and so do I.

The Stranger

Acacias
soft and blue,
feather against gray sky.
White barked trees
rustle in the ascent
of Spring's rush.
A stranger
in the growing dark
among the new greens
finds love
in the pulsing buds.

Moisture at Midday

Purified seawater
pours from the shower head,
smelling like eggs
like sulfur.
Drops
glaze the glass door,
trailing shadows
of themselves,
slithering across the floor
like tadpoles.
Mutton birds
moan outside
the slatted window.
I emerge into heat,
sweat already rolling
down shoulder blades
between breasts.
Shoes laid out to dry
steam
on a wooden bench,
crawling with lizards.

Set Against

Settling in
to a new place
a new home,
but old habits rise
and bubble against the surface of the day;
a bowl of cereal
stolen while standing over the sink
before bed.
Far beyond the morning coffee,
the structure of the day
is built
on rituals of space
on the dance of the routine;
from alarm to toothpaste
to first breath on the stoop
      tinted still with night jasmine
to last light
      yellow gold globe on the ceiling
      fading slowly against closed lids.

      Fading softly
      against branches wreathed in dripping needles
          soft blue grey
          going black against red setting light and grey dusk.

      Fading
      though my mind clings.
      Memory imbued
      with a new value
      against blooming jacaranda.

The scent of pine,
so sharp, so common
pales.

Set Against continues

Song birds no longer cry my awakening
as I adjust to kerrawangs.

New place new home,
but still a bowl of cereal
as a common rain washes away the smog
and mattes the dust on a traveler
settling in.

Another Damned Café

White and rose walls
frame the glass case,
its twelve cakes
sagging on their plates.
two rows of bottles
each a jeweled liquid
a chemical cocktail
for mind and body
lined up,
soldiers
with their labels
at attention,
before the plastic cactus.

Hysteria

Light pulses
red.
The flowers
in their beds
of straight rows
tremble
beneath the cripple limbs
of a downed tree.
The sky
goes black at the edges,
curling in on itself
like a page
on fire.

In the Spirit of Julie Andrews

Woven blankets
with two-inch stripes
tacked above the booths
sombrero hats
straw
braided mats
that bleed green
on wet table tops
fast guitars
big skirts
arroz con pollo
and a salted rim
with extra lime
before the *sopapillas* rise
like clouds
from a honey lake.

Untitled Rayograph

"Spurn not the dreams that come through the Righteous Gate: when righteous dreams come, they have the weight of truth. By night we drift abroad, night frees imprisoned Shades, and even Cerberus casts aside his chains and strays." –Propertius 4.7

shades and shades
of black and white
no grays
but in-betweens
corkscrews on corkscrews
in corkscrews
the Shades
under a wire dome
no chrome
just black in shades
and overlaid with white

A Breath of Grey

The skyline sank into the mist of blue.
The closest trees, tinted green,
the only color eight floors below
touch the morning's dripping face.

Pale light tiptoed across the carpet,
trailing a dull grey glow
that painted corners in shadows
and stole the colors from the furniture.

The palette of rainy mornings hung
but a few moments before retreating
behind bold squares of hot light
that tumble with a thud on a dappled city.

Spider Web

The branch swayed
bare limbs
like whips in the breeze.
Weightless strands of a spider's web
bulged and collapsed
in on themselves
at the mercy
of the tree.
Light shifted twice
splashing the delicate strands
with silver
then concealing
against backlit blue.

The Owl

Matte black branches
leer and breathe
on the far side
of framed glass panes
the hand of winter
slick with ice
tapping slender nightmares
in a gusty wind

Sloped roof of tile
sighs beneath its cap
of checkered whites
moon-silvered snows

A soft whistle
eight steps too low
not human, a lonely bow
to the muffling mantle
of heaping flakes

yellow-gold globes
swivel, taking in
the shiver of light
cold, blue, between the pines

Driving Through Nebraska

The sun always rises red
in these poems.
I don't know why,
but I like that for a beginning.
The sun rises red,
which it actually does out over
a Western plain.
It pulls itself out of the corn stalks
glowing deeper, redder
than it had been
when it set the night before
and stretches its warm pink arms
over the straight roads
and crooked fences.
It blows a soft palette of color
onto a few lingering clouds,
edges the oak leaves in yellow strands
and then dances orange and gold on every stalk
of ripening corn
until finally losing momentum
and settling into a solid blue sky
that goes on forever.

Part II

Return

The Remains of Hazel's Hall

One hundred and six
Northwest Twenty-Second Place
is a house trimmed in blue,
paint peeling from its weathered boards.
In the windows
near the roof,
a ghost floats
prim and pale
behind a diamond pane.
It was number fifty-two
Lucretia Place
when the ghost was a girl.
Eighty years since her passing
only a shimmer
of her pen remains –
a listening macaw,
yellow feathers still bright
against black satin,
perches on a marble stone,
its head tilted toward the trees.

Child on a Swing

Dome wide eyes
as a cerulean sky
an arching, ever open blue.
Straw hair, unruly fields
growing golden by the fall.
Wiry muscles line her arms,
deep and rippled as aspen roots.
The distance of the plains
stretches limbs out in her soul
with breath sweet and musky as the wind.

Return

No matter how far
traveled the spice-filled distances,
there is a spot
that draws us
back to the hills or forests
of our former selves,
to the stone church,
the yard of our childhood
with its timid sprites,
the room within reach of the cherry blossoms
where a first love twice perched
in cool night air to whisper
somber songs.

Reflections

Five chandeliers,
each a wheel of cups,
stretch twenty spiny limbs
across black tiles,
flanked by a dozen pronged sconces
clutching rough brick walls.
Shadowed swan faces
brake into bits on the cutlery,
smeared to a mere palette
of flesh tones on the pitcher,
in the curve of a lemon peel,
in the fleeing grains of salt.

Christmas Lights in March

I see through myself
In the charcoal tinted glass
Ghost-like pale
Hair curling in wisps from my face

Outside parked cars reflect
Strands of Christmas lights
Gold against the black sky
Gray houses

Tawny branches with new pink blooms
Cold coffee slag in my mouth
Gutter radio susurration
Vibrates the glass and my face

Twinkle lights swing gently
Gusting in and out of my skin

Crossing the Desert

I've made this drive a dozen times
from the tree lined drive
out to the highway;
slick charcoal
unrolling between the hills.
Two hours of foothills and ridges.
A plateau marks the switch
to endless grasslands,
rocking and whistling in the air currents
made by the passing cars.
Another half day the landscape changes –
rough cliffs, clouds of red dust,
fierce shrubs lashed to the land.
The desert lasts the distance of a day
right to the mountains,
a barrier to the dusk-tinted sea.

In Response to a Girl Saying She Wasn't Interested in Seeing the US

endless grasses stretching

blue-flower-hands to the ocean

a treeless dessert

low shrubs, burnt sand valleys

cut deep into coarse cliffs

where survivors clung by their fingertips

to a fragile life

conifer stands embrace in purple shade

aspens burst from green to sweet-corn yellow

maples red in September

and the mist swells a song

from the bay to coat the city in its chill

so don't tell me
you're not interested

don't tell me
my country doesn't draw

After reading CK Williams

We have become obsessed with minimalism, the "short-and-sweet,"
the clip, the sound
       bite
We pitter, baby-step, and shuffle. We two-step or triple-step. But
never leap with toes
       pointed and muscles flexed.
Or take long advancing strides across the page, swimming forward
through the deep grasses of a
       dew-wet field.
I think the Latin writers have it right, rambling from thought to
thought, meandering sentences,
     the double folded line,
Allowing the reader, in the faded leather armchair set to catch the
last rays of the
       afternoon sun,
Find their own rhythm in the words, pursuing the story with the pace
of their own heart
  and expansive breath.

Bar 1201

The beat of the music
vibrates the mirrors on the walls
pounds out its rhythm
through flickering drop lights.
The shadow of skirts
parade through the bands
of reflection on the steel bar.
Backlit bottles
poised like soldiers.
Tongues flick,
teeth clack in the dense corners.
I retreat
behind my glass,
my internal turret,
to find myself looking out of looking in.

An Afternoon in the Rocky Mountains

I walked 40 paces
with a shadow of my former self
sang a hymn to remembrance
beneath a resin branch
I found peace and past
in the feathers of the wind
and lounged in the arms
of lost innocence
sure now, my tread on snowy slopes,
I found again the frustrations
of bursting youth
and knew the 40 paces
would walk me
both back and on.

Morning Fog

Morning
sleeps in dew,
covered
in her own breath, mist
clinging
to her rising breasts,
green light on her brow
pulsing
as before a storm.

Alone at night in front of my computer, I contemplate the point of work

Seven hours of sleep
if I go to bed now
and if
I fall asleep immediately
without the languishing in thought
planning the next meeting
writing that last report
that was due yesterday but which got postponed
because marketing wasn't ready
and the guys down in graphics
had the last nine days off.
Six hours and fifty minutes
now
if

but there are a few lines left
to write
on the point of work

Funny how the synonyms of point
are tip
top
apex
and end

the point of work is to reach the top
the tip top
the apex of your intellectual ability moderated by someone else's timeline
the end of self and the beginning of team
the head, who was never the head of the class,
is the one directing the bottom,
who are the only ones who get it,
who see what this policy would really mean

Alone at night ... continues

how this change would spiral
would domino through from training to bus dev
front the front desk to the back office
from the plains to the summit
of the mountain looming above the vast sea of grasses

and so I come to the point
the point of work is sharp
and I'm down to six hours and nine minutes
if I fall asleep immediately.

First Morning

Tawny light
creeps across wet grasses
syrupy and thick at this early hour.
The day has yet to gain momentum.
The air is dense and sweet,
with new blooms
pink buds opening as from a long sleep.
The rain will come
and aluminum skies
crinkled like foil with strips of clouds.
The susurration of traffic
through streams of water
will drown out the birds
and the colors will fade.
But for this first breath of day
the world is a honey pot
golden-hued
and poised for song.

Uriel

Keeper of history –
pity is not my tongue
chosen to watch
record ten rank spans of man –
so you may know
how man grew from suffering
and fell from love.

Hyacinth in Shade

Her face,
camber cheeks
sodden,
clings
to a slender stem
bent with the weight
of rain.
Moon-white palms
bow
to the steady creep
of light.

I hate it when they put stickers on the front of books

James Mackie's Passages
is puckered
from the glue-backed green.
A square stain,
tacky to the touch,
mars the right top corner.
Not the wear of a book well loved,
but of an author forgotten
marked down
by the hand of some long-necked egret.
Mackie's revolution,
his guns drawn on the sonnet,
now devalued
among the gloss.
And how I scrubbed
at the Dakota Incantations!
Like stripping back the bark
to see the grain,
the cover forever dark from finger oil.

Three-day Weekend

Couples cuddle
beneath plum blossoms
clutching at desperation
in a shower of frost-colored petals.
An old man throws a Frisbee
for his speckled dog.
Nanna straightens a rumpled pink dress.
Two women lounge
bikinis beneath a fresh sun,
books covering faces
from the glare.
On the only stretch of green for miles,
people gather under the trees
on blankets
in chairs
to eat cold chicken dinners
and smear their cheeks with watermelon rinds.

Ghosts

There are a host of ghosts
at my door; they knock
the wood from its frame
swinging the door in,
a soupcon of air
bursts quickly through the gap.
Sometimes the door will flutter
before latching to its hinges,
a ghost who's indecisive
about the in and the out.
Another gust
will knock it wide and fast,
air rushing in to rattle the wall hangings
and jumble my hair.
I can just imagine
what he must have been like in life
his broad shoulders filling the doorway.

Sonoma Vacation

1. You stayed in bed until eleven
while I wandered the town
ate local jam
read by the pool
in the Beauty of the Lilies.
Orange buttercups
blanketed the gullies between vineyards,
their rustle brought on feathered air.

2. And we kissed
in the fields
at crossroads
beneath an olive tree
all along a dusty road littered with the stresses
we'd tossed from the open windows
as we wound among the hills.

Final Gift

It is a tiny piece of bone,
cut, perhaps, from an antler,
round and ragged with a ring
like tree bark or a burn
around the edge.
The center has been drilled out
as if by a worm
to form a tiny hole,
now filled with a slither of gold.
It curls out across the short expanse,
seemingly in constant motion,
moving away from a centrifuge –
antlerian vortex.
It swings by a thin chain –
gold boxes knotted together,
roping around fine neck hairs.

It was the last gift she ever gave me,
a farewell when her hands shook too hard
to write a check or sign a card.
You like it? she asked
then *So we're quits.*
Her ivory limbs rattled –
dainty as the chain, ancient as the disc of bone.

Penance

Wearing the new coat
you gave me last night
I am over warm at my desk
office heater cranking out above my head.
But I won't take it off
for the sweat collecting on fine neck hairs
or the pink roses
blooming on cheeks and hands.
The collar where you rubbed your beard
retains a tang of your soap.

Four Bars

Glistening with oil
slick pizzas steam

pale smoke fuses
with grime on the walls

melon pink lipstick
on her mouth, his glass

vision of an age
goggle green

Before I Knew You

I read a story once
about a girl who lost her husband
on the day that they were married.

I read the whole book
all 300 some pages
in an afternoon beneath a willow
on the lawn.

It was before I knew you.

The light was tender
between the leaves
and the air smelled of new earth
turned skyward for a breath
like the earth on that poor husband's grave.

Tonight, while you slept,
I woke to smell that earth
soft as moss and deep.

Valentine's Day 2006

Bits of ice
pelt the hot red petals
of the dozen roses
and frost her bent head
with violent grace.
A slash of sun light
more knife than glow
pierces the bare trees.

Pursued

(for Steve)

Tracking footprints
in sandstone mud
crisp air

now tracking mine
while tracking his

a surge of blood to the throat

I flee
humbled by the deep impression
of toes, claws,
leathery pad in soft clay.

Framed Photo on My Desk

A thick streak of light
like a careless painter's stroke
obscures the brown grasses,
the leafless branches of a sugar maple,
and blurs
the horizon blue
with their blue jeans.
His hat
brown leather bargain
from the Chinatown market
sits tight above the ear.
Her sweatshirt a mimic
of wisps of cotton cloud.
Their fingers interlace
she smiles, he frowns;
glare on his glasses
and her teeth.
My parents rest on a fallen tree
in the light of two winter days.

A Day Off Work

He faked a fall
by the front gate,
slipping on the icy walk,
arms flying up in surprise.
He landed on his hip
heavy with a groan.
A room of suits
ran calculators,
cross-examined numbers,
and sent us home.
Now I'm sitting on the porch,
huddled in a patchwork quilt,
watching the rain dance on parked cars.

It is the Daily Things...

the sweetest sip of coffee
at the bottom of the cup

a favorite pen

a smile from a stranger
that broadens when returned

8:46

Fifteenth phone call for the day
Rhonda at Halliburton
but Dean isn't there
call Brighton – no she doesn't know the number
it's Colorado
so three zero three something
then Joanie
he can't be paged
try this number
another three oh three
Dean is in a meeting
with the techs
that won't be out until lunch
so try back
at two
and all I wanted was a name.

On a Wedding

Bells
silver in the morning dew
ribbon through knoll
and dale
dispersing like threads.

Edges

I am thankful
for the moments of waiting
when we pause in an eddy;
our lives swirling around us,
rushing currents bubbling,
piling up along the edges
of our stillness.
Sound pools,
dark and glossy as a lake at dawn.

Temple

Floors of pale green and silver tiles,
laid like tiny tombstones,
cover the bare earth,
crawl the walls like
lines of mirrored ants,
march up pillars,
stretch around arches.
They reflect the light,
darkening corners,
intensifying shadows
that pool blue behind porticos.
A round fountain
sits in the middle of the courtyard,
gurgling.
Orange and pink petals
dip and nod around the edges of its pool.
Outside indigo doors,
curved and carved like spring blooms,
an old woman squats on a tattered rug,
tea cup sized pots filled with spices
laid out in the mud.

I Have Loved You Even in Darkness

Before you
I loved only in the dark
the lights snuffed
so I need not be myself
so his hands could be any hands
our breath, together,
the breath of many
of any
but ourselves.
But you
I have loved in light
under a hot noon
in the open
my eyes the same way
as our breathing rolled out wheat fields
between our two coasts.
And even in the storms ~
unemployment,
debt,
the long winters of the North ~
the light is on above us
keeping out the chill.

Ancient Song

like a heavy breath,
its rhythms
are sweet with wine,
and dense with wisdom.
I hear an antiphon
soak the pages of our history.
In chanted choices,
I find a voice not my own.

Painting Over the Stairs

On her back in death
One knee bent
An arm behind her head
Coquettish among the grasses
Where her body lies

Her face is turned away
Her chin an arrow
At the backdrop of clouds
Ear cocked as if listening
Black shoes nestle among the blades

Bluegrass, the stems of rushes
Near her still pink ankles
Not gone too long then
When the artist found her
Perched like a bird on the edge

of a life too swiftly lived

Freedom Quilt

Stitched together
the pieces of a quilt
were freedom,
a map to liberty
and life; red squares
of the republic, blue blocks,
stripes of yellow like the fields,
all pointing north
from the river bank,
passed the big oak with a broken limb,
to a barn, weathered and pale,
where the hostler has a blanket
and a place to hide.
From there through the wheat
at night
by speckled triangles
of sky, star led
to a basement or another barn.
Countless nights
broken into bits, rearranged
in memory, stitched together
a patchwork to sovereignty.

A Dusty March

There is a lean contour
between the trees
and the road,
a dusty patch alive with wind
and banded worms,
crusading among the roots
and displaced soil.
A column of ants
makes a pilgrimage.
I share it with them –
the armored beetles,
the pills bugs,
and the flies –
we all make our way
along a thin line
between the wonder and the rush.

Grave

Bones
dissemble in the dirt,
a heap
of forgotten triumph,
hollow and earth burnt.
How vivid green the grass!

Groping in the Dark

That old nightmare
claws,
its teeth
ripping at my limbs.
My flesh turns yellow
like an old bruise
then blisters
until, at last, it bursts,
a fountain of sand
whipping away on the wind,
leaving only my bones
bleached by the heat.

My outstretched hands are white as snow.

Depression

Fog
thick with cedar
green with rotting pine
spreads
from the ditches
to the roads –
curtains closing in on the day.

Walking in high-heeled shoes

The city vibrates through
man made soles,
foam blown thin, arched
leather stretched tight.
The pounding of four million lives
lived in concert
becomes a pin prick,
a point of bright light
at the base of the Achilles
that spreads its tributaries up the calf,
winding and thumping
up the back of the knee,
around tensed thighs
into the core where it fans out
like bamboo bound by painted silk
to wrap the body in layers and leaves –
a coquettish dance between moment and muscle.

Mood Swings

Close to the mountains
storms descend in minutes
wrath unchecked by dampening plains
clouds pile up like foam
at the edge of the sea
going from white fluff to menacing
grey-black-low
snow snapping the flower stems
forcing the trees to grovel
gutters fill with blue-tinted ice
and we're still pulling laundry from the lines.

Sixes

Peppermint by the blue front wall
Sage of the left, growing soft and tall

Parsley and dill paired two to a pot
Thyme creepers on the edge of the plot

Rosemary with her pine-like limbs
Windows thrown open to an herbarium wind.

Sunrise in an Oregon Winter

Freezing rain and hail
were the forecast
for this Wednesday morning –
storm advisory from midnight to midday –
but when the cars began to pull into the lot,
it was still a dry cold grey,
not yet wet
obsidian and musty with saturated dust.
We gathered our belongings –
rain coats and lunches
umbrellas and books –
crawled out of our pods
to stand in confusion
beneath a tiger striped sky.

Haiku

Seasons change to red
Outside my leaded window
Inside I am blue

Lead crawls a pale weight
Liquid stone filling the veins
Autumn plagues the trees

Globes shifted by wind
Green bells chiming in the mind
A gardener's psalm

Pastoral hearts beat
In orange flesh, pale seeds
Roasted fruits of fall

Common Image

The moon hung high
bright
as an eye
over the dusty summit of Mt Hood.
The purple sky
reflected cobalt on the snow.
A plume of flakes
billowed in a cold wind
from the tip of the peak,
mimicking the dark shadows on the partial sphere above.
I sat and gazed at the vision,
glowing in soft light, behind the icons of my computer screen.

Our Winter

The curve of your back is red
from lying in front of the heater,
the floor's impression
tiger striped across your cheek.
Knees tucked inside your shirt,
which I borrowed from the laundry pile,
I cling to a cup of tea,
socks on my hands.
The phone rings. Both heads turn.
It is outside the kitchen
outside the reach
of the gas heater, wall mounted,
facing the stove.
We let it ring,
shift our feet on the hardwood.
Ice collects on the window sill.

Oral Histories

From the basement window of your office
you can just see the street at eye level
cars rush by, six wide
flashing their headlights through the rain

the dappled light on the right wall
reminds you of that hike in Bandelier
four months and forever ago
when the camera broke in the parking lot

we had to work hard to remember
telling each other stories
about the satin feel of the wood rails
as I climbed up to peer at a stamped dirt floor

a blackened ceiling, a carving, like Chaco,
of us/them with hands held high and wide
my heart in my throat to see myself there
reaching out to this cliff life, so close to the sky

and you tell me about the blue winking between green leaves
the flutter of our hair as we ascend from the kiva
choking on dirt the Boy Scouts stirred up
brushing each other off, wiping hands on pants

gritty water on our faces, in our mouths
until red light tells us both to go back
that the day has ended, the traffic has stopped
sunset blinks into pieces on a right hand wall

On Leaving Montana

A night champaign,
tressed black and thick
against a sky of barely blue,
waves its thousand arms,
spreads its hair
across the pillows of the earth.
The chuckle of wheat chaff
rolls out from the hills,
a supple rushing in the wind.
At the edge of vision,
purple mounts rise from the fields
sentries to a winsome nightfall.

Boomerang

Winter has arrived
in a black glove,
sticky with rubber beads
so it will hold the wheel.

I found it in the pocket of my coat,
clinging to the acetate lining.
The first day for a glove.
How strange to find the sky so blue.

Along the roads
the leaves are rotting
in piles;
puce like Pennyroyal.

Upslope fog
on the drive home.
Oblique funnels of ice
hanging from the gutters.

Twenty five days
until the solstice
when the sun,
driven from our faces,

begins its boomerang,
three months of cold
waiting for the two-way Airbender.
Turuwal fire-starter.

Baja Temple

Cacti
raise steeples
like ancient temples
among the rocks.
Wind muffled
by the blue-gray horizon
of dusk.

May 22nd

The streets are flooding
with spring rain,
carrying a fleet of debris
down rushing gutters.
Dull shadows edge the hills,
a line of sentries to the storm.
Leaves show their undersides
to the whipping,
pale
but paler still
against wet-black bark.
A woman stands beneath an awning
her red coat
a bright spot on the day.

Storm at Dante's Bar

Maracas
in her white hands,
blur against the dark.
Her heat, a drum beat
between her thighs,
that echoes in their eyes
as she sings
in a voice part honey part sting.

6:52 AM

On the crackled edge of dawn
beyond the fractured light
a circle of dark
hovers,
halo's shadow,
sun stalker,
a storm's storm.
Bits of daylight
flash through its wings,
bright knives through the feathers.
A red smudge
creeps across the belly
of a cloud bank.
The tips of blue grass blades
drip honey colored dew
onto my pant legs,
morning soaking into my skin.

Tuscan Picnic

The courtyard is a circle
of hanging blooms;
crimson globes backlit by dewy light
against the rough gold of adobe
arched walls and the rust sloping
sun burnt roof.
The Bells of Ireland
ring foreign as Moluccella.
Bobbing gently below the eaves
Narcissus Ziva,
a Tuscan white at the edge
of a sandstone patio.
A wood lattice
hangs heavy with vines
over whicker furniture,
blue ceramic pitcher,
and two cups ~ half empty ~
dripping condensation on bare legs.

Telemon

I have a telemon
supporting my heart.
His head is a marble sphere
bedecked in waves of tresses
that sits upon shoulders
sloped and wide as the plains.
His hands
are held aloft
as in supplication.
Beneath a chest like a drum
his heart beats
a thump thump
to the rhythm of my own keening.
If only his legs
extended through my own
I would still be standing
gallant in my grief.

You Forget

how white the air can get,
in a snow storm
how glutinous
and how the cold thrashes.
B'hemot,
his nose pierceth through snares;
the unconquerable beast
cloaked in wisps and petals,
his bridal pale deceives
the sharp edges of his claws.

Sunday Breakfast

sugar crystals glitter in the foam
of a half-full cup
woodsmoke wafts with the rain
in a window I propped open with a glass
eggs feathered with milk
tart tomatoes, sweet ham
and still smelling of sleep
your toothpaste kisses on my neck

Winter Fruit

On a day this cold,
grey light and damp,
snow spreading its fingers
across the eaves,
I plant my garden.
I smell the broken earth
beneath the watermelon vines
and feel the spiny leaves
of zucchini prick my thumbs.
Berries rupture between my teeth.
The chives blossom, nodding their purple heads.

The Day's Complexion

A swarthy wash,
freckled before the dawn
blooms to a blush –
a child's rosy cheeks
blood rushing just beneath the skin.

Strange Place for a Postcard

Pin straight rows of grapes
edged across a low hill
in the middle of the postcard.
Dense gullies filled with bent apple trees,
yellow tulips, and reedy grass
framed the little vineyard
like a border on a glimpse of paradise.
It was out of place,
that postcard,
tacked up on the grey pressboard
on the outside of her cube.
Why not on the inside
facing the desk
where a quick look up from the computer screen
would be gifted with green hills under the yellow light?
Why there
in the thin space between two cubes
not large enough for a person to stand
where only it can only be seen by sitting sideways,
back to the computer and the walkway?
I can only guess.
Perhaps it fell from her desk
after hours or on a busy day
and she didn't notice,
so the janitors picked it up
but couldn't throw it away,
that glimpse of paradise too good for the garbage,
so they hung it up where there was space
above the boxes of printer paper –
a tiny dream hanging beneath the ductwork and the dim.

An Ending

A purple leaf
clings to its final breath
on bare branches
and taps the grimy window
with its paper edge.

Veinte Cinco de Augusto

Un dia de lluvia
despues un verano mas calor;
alivio
como el rio
romperando de una presa.
Hojas de los sicómoros
giran amarillo
en los bordes ~
lengua del combio.
Mi alma rompo
de los vinculantes
como el rio
como la lluvia ~
ondear,
la hoja primera
ambrazando el otoño.

Twenty-Fifth of August

One day of rain
after a hot summer;
relief
like a river
breaking from a dam.
The leaves from the sycamore
go yellow
at the edges ~
language of change.
My soul breaks
from its bindings
like the river
like the rain ~
to flutter,
the first leaf
embracing the fall.

Thursday

The noise outside
is seeping in,
taking up the space
where my thoughts should be,
stacking up
like books on overloaded shelves
leaning
helter-skelter
shoved in sideways
piled one on top of the other
and I am bowing
wood beneath the weight.

A House for Johnny

I saw a house today
that made me think of you;
a Tuscan style villa
on a lakefront winding road,
wrought iron balconies,
and sunset stucco walls.
It wasn't you,
too neat, too dense
too rich, too closed.
But the honeysuckle bloomed
and I thought of us as kids
plucking blossoms
to sweeten our tongues
on the white marble library steps.
A woodpecker,
red capped and barred,
brushed its wing tips
on the cherry buds.
A motor boat thrummed
along the farthest shore.
Wood smoke rose blue and pale
from the house next door.
A chickadee in a nearby pine
and I could smell again
vanilla bark and thistle
and raisins in a box
over-warm from my pocket and the sun.

Coffee Shop on Wednesday When I Really Should be at Work

Three computers
two books
five coffees
and I am back to my obsession.
Two continents
five States
three years
and nothing to show
but a pile of mail –
all No Thank You,
Keep Trying,
Maybe Next Time,
so I am here,
four others and our coffees,
a barista and a dream.

Days of the Week

I met him on a Saturday
in an Irish pub
by the window
where the corner booth
intersects the street
and the smooth wood bar.
The glass pint slid
in its pool of water
when he stretched out his hand.
I gave him my number
on a Thursday
over my French toast and tea.
He took me to dinner
on a Monday.
I kissed him
on a Wednesday,
the metal handle
of my driver's side door
pressed into my back,
the taste of hesitance
still thick upon our lips.
I told him that I loved him
on a Friday,
my fingers grasped
between his,
the early hours of the morning
fast approaching.
I became addicted to him by Sunday
and someday,
perhaps a Tuesday,
we will declare it a good week.

In This Little Bit of Space

between the elbows
and the beers
at most alone –
a breath of stillness,
a petal
caught beneath the twisting tree.

Forest Path

Among the wild lilies
I found death
the death that is not an end
but a beginning,
a resurfacing of air from the depths of a green pond,
smelling of the rebirth of centuries.
The dropping needles, crunching and snapping,
mark my progress
from my time to another time ~
a past
belonging to the then and the now,
remembered in the chickadee's song,
calling to the dusk,
and the tendril of a vine,
creeping from the foliage of a distant fall.
Time in the forest stops
and crawls
and bounds and circles.
All pasts become one past.
All presents become one present.
Here they are borne upon a hot wind
through new grey-green needles
only to merge
ends to their beginnings, teeth to tales ~
a convergence among the pines.

Messages

One bush, waist high, is in bloom.
The smell permeates the block
and the block between.
It follows me to my office
through the rain
like a ghost and hangs
behind my eyes
a curtain keeping out the mute slate sky.
Today I stuck my nose into wet pale petals
in an act of faith.
A leaf drenched with green
and firm, fell hours later from my hair.

Storm

On wings of a death angel,
a cry like a dirge;
adjure the blessings of the green earth.
Ridged with mountains,
caressed with seas,
home is a canyon
deep, and pungent, and blue.

I am life
Leaving,
my heels gauging tracks through the sodden fields.

After Your Next Promotion

The house is on a dead end block
with seven houses lopped around
a kidney bean shaped street.
The yard is small and square,
flagstones cutting paths from door
to street and street to fence.
Daffodils and hyacinths
checker narrow earth-filled beds,
a breath above the grass,
and line the edges of the porch,
where the swing creaks and sways.
A wind chime made of shells,
collected on our last trip to the sea,
clinks a vacant tune.
Paint is peeling from the eves
and the doorknob rattles in the wind,
but the windows open to a kitchen,
yellow with light and laughter.

Absolution Tea

The middle shelf
holds three antique tea pots –
round brass like a moon,
square white ceramic,
Blue enamel with a half-crest handle.

The Snare of the Hunter
leans wearily against A Memoir.
Three Tibetan statues top the case,
flanked by photos of Sonoma vines.
The whole wall from floor to ceiling

ripples with rings of reflected
copper light.
No cutting corners in a Sleigh,
but here we sit, cups steaming,
bindings straining against our palms.

I Have a Favorite Word

Carapace
a turtle's home
the armor for a tiger beetle
metal green with bands or drips
of gold across the back,
a blackened mollusk cup
lined with satin sheets of pink,

the casing, covering, shield, or crust
that keeps the soul inside.

First Page

The cover of this notebook
is yellow
like restaurant butter
dyed with carrot juice,
buttery like the inside of a croissant.
I haven't even paid for it yet
and I'm writing in it.
I stood for twenty minutes
or more, perhaps,
to choose it

from among the gloss
green and black
and bubblegum pink
journals for every fetish –
too small for poems,
too big for my bag,
too bright and clean –
without earth stains
from that camping trip up north,
a spilled mug of St Laurent,
water from the leak you still haven't fixed.

I dropped it
dented the cover –
not so daunting now
not so white and fresh
but like laundry on the line smelling new but possessed.

I want yet another tea pot

They hold, it seems to me,
infinite promise
for small moments of peace;
a smile shared through steam
a blossoming flower on the coldest day.

Bio

Molly Weller was born in Boulder, CO in the middle of the night, during a wind storm, and spent her youth running wild in the foothills of the Rocky Mountains. She now lives on the side of a hill in Portland, OR, where she runs wild through the Columbia Gorge. She holds degrees from Willamette University, the University of Colorado, and the University of Sydney. She leaves a little piece of her heart in every place she visits.

She got her start as a writer with a ghost story contest she won at the age of nine. She is now a college English instructor. Her work has been published in both the United States and Australia.

Printed in the United States
130781LV00003B/2/P